What's in the Backyard?

by Carmel Reilly

CONTENTS

OXFORD
UNIVERSITY PRESS
AUSTRALIA & NEW ZEALAND

FULL OF LIFE

Backyards might seem like quiet places but they are full of life. They are home to all kinds of tiny animals.

Some of these animals, like earthworms, ants, beetles and centipedes, live on the ground. Others, like spiders, snails, cicadas and stick insects, are found among the plants. Flies, wasps, butterflies and mosquitoes move through the air.

ON THE GROUND

Earthworms

Earthworms live in soil, in **leaf litter** on top of the soil, and under rocks and logs.

Earthworms have **segmented** bodies. On each segment there are four pairs of small **bristles**. These bristles help earthworms to move through the soil.

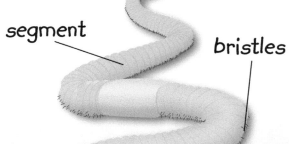

segment

bristles

Ants

Ants live in **colonies** in soil, in rotten logs and around buildings.

Ants are insects, so they have three main body parts – a head, a **thorax** and an **abdomen**. Worker ants use their jaws to grip their food.

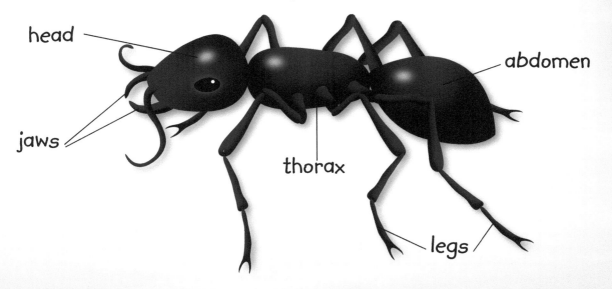

head

jaws

thorax

abdomen

legs

Beetles

Beetles can be found in soil, in flowers and in leaf litter.

Beetles are insects. They have two pairs of wings. One pair of wings acts like a hard shell around the body. The other pair is often used for flying. Beetles have strong back legs for walking and running.

thorax

wings

legs

abdomen

centipedes

Centipedes can be found in soil, in leaf litter or under rocks and logs. Some may even go into houses.

legs

segment

Centipedes have segmented bodies. The word centipede means "100 legs". However, most centipedes have fewer than 100 legs. Each segment of their bodies has a pair of legs.

AMONG THE PLANTS

Snails

Snails live on garden plants. They eat leaves, stems, bark and **algae**.

A snail's shell helps to protect its body and stops it from drying out. Snails have a big "foot" underneath their shell that contains muscles that help them move along. The foot also produces slime that makes moving easier.

shell

"foot"

spiders

Spiders can be found around trees, bushes, old logs and buildings.

Spiders have two body segments and eight legs. Not all spiders make webs, but they all make silk. The silk is used to climb, build **egg sacs** and trap **prey**.

legs

abdomen

head

cicadas

Cicadas can be found in trees, bushes and grass.

Cicadas are insects with two pairs of wings and mouthparts that pierce and suck. An adult male cicada makes a high-pitched sound using drum-like **membranes** on its abdomen.

thorax

wings

mouth

abdomen

head

legs

stick insects

Stick insects can be found in eucalypt trees, rose bushes and fruit trees.

Stick insects have thin, long or flat bodies that look like sticks, stems or leaves. This helps them to hide from **predators**. Most stick insects are green or brown. Some stick insects have brightly coloured wings that can only be seen when they fly.

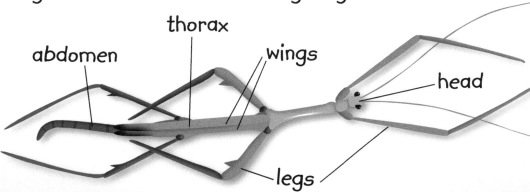

abdomen

thorax

wings

head

legs

IN THE AIR

Flies

Flies spend most of their time near rubbish and rotting food.

Flies are insects with two wings. They have tiny hairs all over their bodies that help them to feel, smell and taste. They suck up food with their mouthparts.

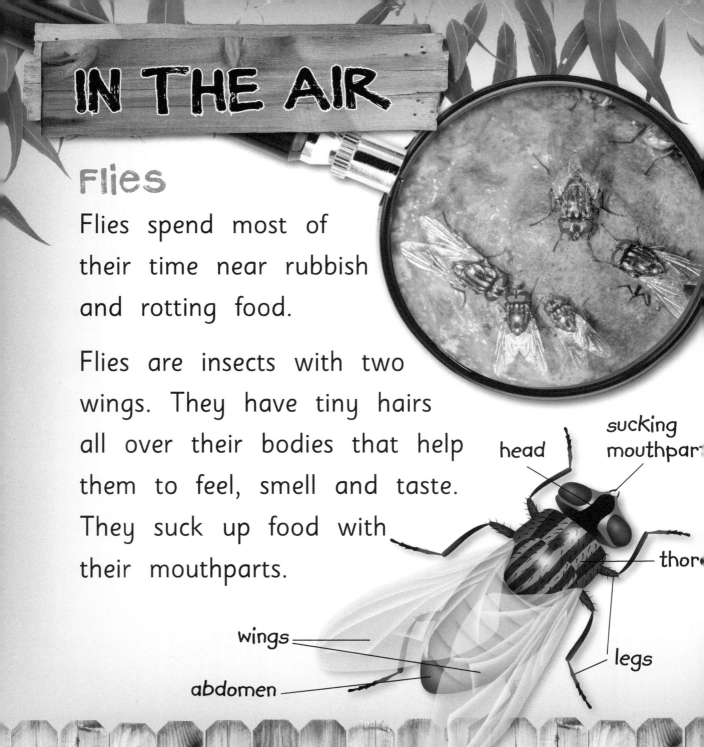

head

sucking mouthpar[t]

thor[ax]

legs

wings

abdomen

Wasps

Wasps make nests in trees, logs, spaces in walls and sometimes in the ground.

There are many different kinds of wasps. A European wasp has yellow and black stripes on its abdomen, with black spots on each yellow stripe. It also has two pairs of clear wings, black **antennae** and a stinger.

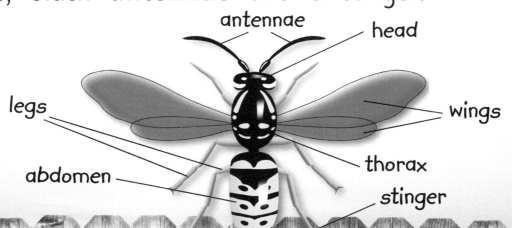

antennae

head

legs

wings

abdomen

thorax

stinger

Butterflies

Butterflies fly from place to place, feeding on **nectar** from flowers.

Butterflies have two pairs of wings, eyes and long antennae. They also have long, tube-like mouthparts to suck up nectar. Butterflies' wings and bodies are covered in tiny scales. These scales are often brightly coloured.

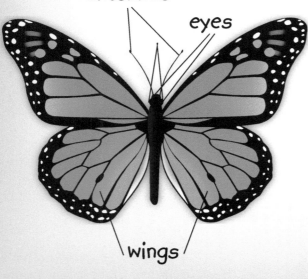

antennae

eyes

wings

Mosquitoes

Mosquitoes rest in cool, dark places during the day but come out at night to feed.

Mosquitoes are insects that feed on nectar from plants. The females of some mosquito species also suck blood. They have long, sharp mouthparts to bite through skin and suck out blood.

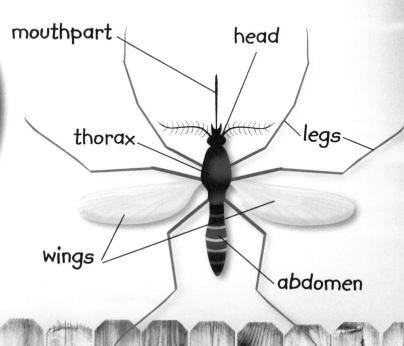

mouthpart

head

thorax

legs

wings

abdomen

GLOSSARY

abdomen   the rear segment of an insect

algae   water plants without stems or flowers

antennae   feelers on the heads of insects

bristles   short stiff hairs

colonies   a group of animals living together

egg sacs   bag-like containers with a membrane that some animals store their eggs in

leaf litter   dead leaves, twigs and plants that have fallen on the ground

membranes   thin linings

nectar   the sweet liquid inside flowers

predators   animals that hunt and eat other animals

prey   animals that are hunted and eaten by other animals

segmented   divided into parts

thorax   the segment of an insect's body between the head and abdomen